DRIVEN

— *by the* —

SPIRIT

DRIVEN

by the

SPIRIT

t r salzer

ARPress
ILLUMINATING IDEAS,
EMPOWERING VOICES

ARPress
45 Dan Road Suite 5
Canton MA 02021

Hotline: 1(888) 821-0229
Fax: 1(508) 545-7580

Ordering Information:
Quantity sales. Special discounts are available on quantity purchases by corporations, associations, and others. For details, contact the publisher at the address above.

Printed in the United States of America.

ISBN-13: Softcover   979-8-89356-315-3
          eBook   979-8-89356-316-0

Library of Congress Control Number: 2024904479

CONTENTS

This book is dedicated to Jesus Christ my Lord and Savior, King and Friend.

Special Thank you to Ken Braun, Mark Rein, and John Zarte and all the Christian brothers and sisters who taught, inspired and encouraged me in my life and this project.

Special appreciation to my father, Carl Romansky, long time copy editor for the Cleveland Plain Dealer, who edited this book with loving devotion to the written word.

PROLOGUE

I was sitting in my Life Group. The topic was journaling. The members of the group were discussing the benefits of this spiritual discipline. As I listened, I could not help thinking *I don't want anyone to read my thoughts.* I have always been very introverted. It is not in my nature to share my private thoughts with others. My friend Rich stated "if someone were to read my journal, they would discover my faith story. What is the harm in that?" Okay, I suppose that is a reasonable argument for keeping a journal. However, the idea still made me feel uncomfortable.

While driving from the Life Group to work, I was contemplating the discussion and pretty much decided journaling was not for me. Suddenly, a thought came into my head out of nowhere. *You need to write a book.* "No," I said. "I don't have time for that." The thought persisted, *You need to write a book.* No, I don't want to write a book.

It is too big an undertaking. *You need to write a book.* Okay, I will write a book.

The following Saturday, I sat down and began writing my thoughts in longhand. I wrote for four hours nonstop! The topic was my personal plan for using everyday activities to strengthen my relationship with God. I have always believed that this plan was private (between myself and God). I never had any intention to share it with others. As I was writing, however, I began to think that perhaps I have something to say that will be valuable to others. I realize, not every Christian will be ready to take on this challenge and that is okay. I believe that we are all at different levels of faith, and if you are not ready to accept this undertaking, I believe the spirit will let you know. Let me be clear, I do not consider myself to be better than those who are not ready. I believe that every one of us is exactly where God wants us to be in our faith walk.

How will you know if you are ready? You must ask yourself the following questions:

- Do I believe my life is too easy?
- Do I crave a closer relationship with God?

- Am I willing to make my life more difficult to improve my relationship with God?

If the answer is yes to all three, then perhaps this plan is for you. If not, do not be discouraged. I am confident that God will guide you to where He wants you to be. And when or if you become ready to take on the challenge, He will let you know. God tends to put desires into our hearts to guide us to His will. I never imagined that I would become passionate about writing a book. And yet, here I am.

Chapter 1

THE CHALLENGE

Now the whole world had one language and a common speech. As people moved eastward, they found a plain in Shinar and settled there. They said to each other, "Come let's make bricks and bake them thoroughly." They used brick instead of stone, and tar for mortar. Then they said "Come let us build ourselves a city, with a tower that reaches to the heavens, so that we may make a name for ourselves;

otherwise we will be scattered over the face of the whole earth."

But the Lord came down to see the city and the tower people were building. The Lord said "If as one people speaking the same language they have begun to do this, then nothing they plan to do will be impossible for them" (Genesis 11:1–6).

John (not his real name) proclaimed in his Bible study group, "I am a good man. I sometimes wonder why bad things happen in my life." The group concluded that it is just the way it is sometimes. As I study the Bible, it occurs to me that in the history of mankind, there has been no time that is easier or more pleasant than living in the United States in the twenty-first century. Of course, there are problems. There is sin in the world. I am not saying that life is perfect. I am not perfect. But if I were to compare my life to those who have lived before me, I cannot help but be in awe of the amazing blessings God has bestowed on my generation and that of those who will come after me. When I think about how humans have lived on this earth for centuries without television, telephones, automobiles, modern plumbing, and electricity, it dumbfounds me. Yet, despite all that we have, we are a generation of whiners.

This is as close to utopia as humans have ever been since the fall. It seems to me that we not only take for granted all that we have, but we tend to complain if there is the slightest malfunction in our technologically advanced way of life. How do I react to a dropped call on my cell phone or when my satellite dish loses a signal? Mild annoyance. How do I react if my car breaks down or the electricity goes out? Moderate frustration. How would I feel if a computer glitch erased all my hard work or someone's stupidity caused damage to my property? Anger. Are we so dependent on modern technology that we are useless without it? Of course not! I am not embracing a position for living off the grid, but rather learning to appreciate our lives as they are. We need an attitude of gratitude. Is it really reasonable to expect life to give us everything we think we deserve?

> *For by the grace given me I say to every one of you: Do not think of yourself more highly than you ought, but rather think of yourself with sober judgment, in accordance with the faith God has*

distributed to each of you (Romans 12:3).

Who decides what we deserve? In the world view, each individual decides what they believe they deserve. In the opinion of the car companies, they decide based on financial status. In the government's view, the majority or the most powerful among us determines what we deserve. In God's view...uh-oh. For those of us who profess that Christ died for our sins, we know that He paid the price for our transgressions and have confidence that our sins will not be held against us. While this is true, it does not absolve us from the responsibility to grow our faith. We need to challenge ourselves to increase our reliance on God in our everyday lives.

> *During the days of Jesus' life on earth he offered up prayers and petitions with fervent cries and tears to the one who could save him from death, and he was heard because of his reverent submission. Son though he was, He learned obedience from what he suffered and, once made perfect, he became the source of eternal*

salvation for all who obey him (Hebrews 5:7).

So, how do we grow our reliance on God? We need to suffer to learn obedience. While it may be counterintuitive to seek suffering, it is necessary to avoid complacency and to mature our faith. The suffering I am referring to is simply self-denial—putting the needs of others ahead of our own needs. Isn't that exactly what Christ did for us and expects us to do as well? Even though it is good and noble to give your time and money to charity, this is not the suffering I am referring to. This self-denial must be felt either physically or emotionally to truly be suffering. There cannot be any hidden agenda (tax-break, pride, or fellowship building). I am not saying these things are wrong, they have their place especially for the Christians who are already struggling in their everyday lives. I am saying that if the goal is faith-building, there cannot be any other motivation other than total reliance on God through suffering.

Be careful not to practice your righteousness in front of others to be seen by them. If you do, you will have no reward from your father in heaven...so that your giving may be in secret. Then your Father who sees what is done in secret, will reward you (Matthew 6:1, 4).

The following proposal is a plan for using self-denial in everyday modern life for the sole purpose of growing total reliance on God. The following guidelines were developed to ensure that the motivation remains pure. The challenge of suffering for spiritual maturity must be done in secret. It needs to be personal between yourself and God. It must be difficult (nearly impossible), so that success can only be achieved by the help of God. It should be clear, so that failure is evident. It should be daily, so that you create a habit of relying on God consistently. And it must be righteous and in accordance with the Scriptures (no self-injurious behaviors). While not every reader will be ready to accept the challenge, I am confident that there are those who, like myself, are craving a closer relationship with God.

Anyone who lives on milk, being still an infant, is not acquainted with the teachings about righteousness. But solid food is for the mature, who by constant use have trained themselves to distinguish good from evil. Therefore, let us move beyond the elementary teachings about Christ and be taken forward to maturity (Hebrews 5:13–14, Hebrews 6:1).

Chapter 2

THE ARGUMENT

Then the Lord said to Satan, *"Have you considered my servant Job? There is no one on earth like him; he is blameless and upright, a man who fears God and shuns evil." "Does Job fear God for nothing?" Satan replied. "Have you not put a hedge around him and his household and everything he has? You have blessed the work of his hands, so that his flock and herds are spread throughout the land. But now stretch out your hand and strike everything he has, and he will surely curse you to your face"* (Job 1:9–11).

Some Christians believe that because they are Christians and try to be good, God has rewarded them with good things in their lives. While it may be true that God does give us many good things, not every Christian is so blessed. We must be careful not to regard the good things in our lives as proof that we are good, only that God is good. Throughout history we know that there have been many faithful Christians who were persecuted, tortured, and killed. In the story of Job, Satan challenges God with the idea that Job was a righteous man only because he was protected by God. Satan is sure that Job would turn against God if all he has was taken away. God knew that Job was a faithful man who would not turn against him no matter what Satan threw at him. God knew Job's heart. God knows our hearts. He loves us anyway.

> *The seed that fell among the thorns stands for those who hear, but as they go on their way they are choked by life's worries, riches and pleasures, and they do not mature* (Luke 8:14).

I find it interesting that Jesus included *riches and pleasures* in his warning. He is telling us that we must be careful not to allow the good things in our lives to stunt our spiritual maturity. For some, the good things in life are proof that God loves us. For others, they believe the good things in life are proof we don't need God in our lives to have good things.

So why do bad things happen? When we think of ourselves as children of God, we tend to imagine ourselves as small children—dependent and trusting. I think a better analogy would be to think of ourselves as adolescents. Anyone who has raised a child to adulthood can understand the dilemma of wanting our children to become independent, successful members of society, but realizing as they make their way in the world they will make mistakes. They will get hurt. God did not create us as robots programmed for total obedience. He knows that we will make poor choices as we grow. We will face trials and we will, at times, question His love for us. Just as the parent of an adolescent, God wants us to come to Him for advice, consolation, and love. He wants us to remember all He has taught us, all He has done for us, and how much He loves us. He wants our love and devotion in spite of the hardships we face or successes we achieve. When I think about those who don't believe they need God in their lives, I think about the lonely widow who sits in her home day after day, hoping for the moment when her child will call or come to see her. Some never will. How sad is that!

> *Therefore I will boast all the more gladly about my weaknesses, so that Christ's power may rest on me. That is why, for Christ's sake, I delight in my weaknesses, in insults, in hardships, in persecutions, in difficulties. For when I am weak, then I am strong* (2 Corinthians 12:9–10).

The Apostle Paul had physical challenges which he refers to *as a thorn in my flesh*. Paul attributed his suffering to a *messenger of Satan* to torment him. All of us, at some time in our lives, will have to deal with health issues. These infirmities promise to become greater as we age. The human body was not designed to face the hardships of life without breaking down. We can attempt to stave off this breakdown of human tissue with diet and exercise, but eventually, it catches up to all of us. (I believe aging is God's way of making us emotionally ready to come home.) It is in our best interest to prepare ourselves to be spiritually ready to suffer the consequences of our aging bodies. The point is that suffering is part of the human condition. We can choose to ignore this fact (until we can't), or as Paul said:

> *Therefore, I do not run like someone running aimlessly; I do not fight like a boxer beating the air. No, I strike a blow to my body and make it my slave so that after I have preached to others, I myself will not be disqualified for the prize* (1 Corinthians 9:27).

So what Paul is saying, first, we need to learn to control our behavior through challenges—the challenge of denying the ego (self). Secondly, if we learn to rely on God, we will be rewarded. The challenge is to merge our spiritual life and our everyday, routine life into one (mind, body, and spirit). This is done by deliberately raising the standard to nearly impossible. By deliberately making things difficult for our minds and bodies, we grow our reliance on God. We become more mindful of Him in our everyday lives.

No discipline seems pleasant at the time, but painful. Later on, however, it produces a harvest of righteousness and peace for those who have been trained by it (Hebrews 12:11).

Chapter 3

THE PROPOSAL

"But just as he who called you is holy, so be holy in all you do" (1 Peter 1:15).

Most of us never really consider travel time as an important aspect of our time here on earth, even though many of us spend more time on the road than we do in church. It was what I considered to be the *in-between* time. After all, nothing very important happens while we are cruising down the highway or stuck in traffic. It is just a *pause* in the action, as we make our contributions to the world. It is the time in-between all the important things we need to do or places we need to be.

Scripture tell us to be holy in all we do. So how do we make this *in-between* time holy? Often while driving, I would contemplate where I was going or what I needed to do when I got there. I never really thought much about the journey itself. I might think about how to get somewhere or how long it would take to get there. GPS pretty much takes care of those issues for me now. Sometimes I would ponder what I needed to do when I arrived at my destination. How would I serve my clients? What will I make for dinner? Other times, I would contemplate the interactions that occurred at the place I was leaving. How could that have gone better? What should I do the next time I see that person? I didn't really give too much consideration to the spiritual side of driving.

We live in an era of multitasking. So much so that we need reminders not to text and drive. The act of driving tends to be a bit mundane, almost to the point of feeling like a waste of time. I decided I needed to find a way to make this *in-between* time more productive. After all, when I add up the minutes I spend driving at the end of an eight hour workday, it usually totals over two hours.

Some days I would become increasingly stressed while driving, especially if I was running late for an appointment or if I was tired and it had been a long day. It is much worse if traffic is particularly heavy due to an accident, construction, or bad weather. I find a particularly long drive can give a person a sense of total helplessness. After all, I have important things to do, and here I sit in my car, waiting for others to get out of my way!

Whatever you do, work at it with all your heart, as working for: the Lord, not for human masters (Colossians 3:23).

It occurs to me that Moses spent a good portion of his life wandering around and never actually reached his destination! That tells me that in God's eyes, the journey is just as important as the getting there. Driving is very much a part of my work. I need to find a way to allow God to guide my journey, to learn what He wants to teach me, and to trust Him alone. In other words, I need to adjust my attitude about my drive time. So, getting back to Moses—forty years! Can you imagine traveling anywhere for forty years? It kinda puts that traffic jam into perspective, doesn't it?

After I have taken a look at how the task is being performed, I need to establish goals and come up with a plan to achieve those goals. Since I am physically trapped inside my car, I need to establish goals that I can achieve without requiring too much physical movement. Since my mind needs to concentrate on the act of driving, I need goals that will not interfere with my ability to attend to the world around me. I decided that perhaps using this time to work on improving my spiritual skills is the way to go. So, what spiritual skills can I sharpen while on the road? Self-control, patience, kindness, and love come to mind, but above all else, putting God first in the process.

I believe that humans have an abundant capacity to learn to control their own behavior. It is not something that comes naturally, though. It needs to be practiced. I hear people say that they would like to learn to be more patient or loving or kind. I don't know if they are actively doing anything to make that happen, but if not, chances are, they won't wake up one day and suddenly be the kind of person they want to be. I have decided to test my theory and challenge myself to use the in-between time during the day to practice these skills.

> *Finally brothers and sisters, whatever is true, whatever is noble, whatever is right, whatever is pure, whatever is lovely, whatever is admirable-if anything is excellent or praise-worthy-think about such things* (Colossians 4:8).

Before I can work on my behavior, I need to change my attitude about my drive time. I need to recognize it as a valuable time in my day. The first step in changing my attitude about driving is to surround myself with reminders of who I am in the universe. I am a child of God. As such, I have a responsibility to behave in a manner that is pleasing to Him. The human brain is easily distracted by negative unholy thoughts. I need to use my senses to remind me of the greatness of our God. I have a wooden cross hanging from my rearview mirror. This visual cue helps to bring my mind back to what is important, and gives me a sense of peace when I start to feel stressed. I always try to listen to Christian music when I am driving. It is difficult to feel stressed when singing praises to the Lord. God has given us a wonderful gift in music. It is said that music soothes the savage beast. Believe me, I have seen that beast in my car when I am driving alone. Christian music always soothes my soul.

> *He makes me lie down in green pastures, He leads me beside quiet waters, He refreshes my soul. He guides me along the right paths for His name sake* (Psalm 23:2–3).

As often as possible, I try to take a drive through the park. To observe the natural world God created is like seeing a glimpse of heaven. There is a sense of wonder and awe in seeing the beauty God created. To associate that feeling with the act of driving gives me a sense of peace and tranquility in the car.

The second step I have used to change my attitude about driving is to learn to respect the act of driving itself. I remember in driver's education, the instructor began by saying "Driving is not a right, it's a privilege." Privileges are generally earned. I did not invent the internal combustion engine. As a matter of fact, I don't even know how it works. God did give mankind the intelligence and vision to create the automobile and mass produce them. And because He did, I could learn to operate a car and learn the laws related to driving in my state, even if I don't always obey them. I, therefore, earned the privilege to drive, not only in Ohio but anywhere else for that matter.

Sometimes I think that if God wanted us to travel at sixty, seventy, eighty-five (Texas) mph, he would have given us wings. Could any of the biblical figures—Old and New Testament—have ever conceived the notion of the automobile? After all, they, for the most part, traveled on foot. Could you imagine in our fast-paced way of life, traveling only on foot? It is inconceivable to me that I could accomplish anything without my car. I am so dependent on my car that I have to go for walks as a recreational and fitness activity. I realize, therefore, not only should I respect the act of driving, but consider it not a right or privilege, but an amazing blessing every time I start the engine.

"I have a right to do anything," you say—but not everything is beneficial. "I

have the right to do anything"—but not everything is constructive. No one should seek their own good, but the good of others (1 Corinthians 10:23–24).

My proposal is simply this—I will, from this point forward, challenge myself to drive like a Christian. I will follow the laws and show kindness to others, to respect the act of driving, and to be grateful for my ability to arrive at my destination safely.

Chapter 4

THE PLAN

Do you not know that in a race all the runners run, but only one gets the prize? Run in such a way as to get the prize. Everyone who competes in the games goes into strict training. They do it to get a crown that will not last, but we do it to get a crown that will last forever (1 Corinthians 9:24–25).

Someone once told me that the police will not stop you for going five to eight mph over the speed limit. I don't know if that is true or not, but

I have never gotten a ticket for speeding within those parameters. Let's talk about what the words *speed limit* mean. It is not a recommended speed or suggested speed (unless it is a yellow sign). The speed limit is the fastest rate of speed allowed by law. Yes, I know this a very painful concept, but driving twenty-six mph in a twenty-five mph zone is speeding. It was pointed out to me in a Bible study many years ago that speeding is a sin. Ouch! Yes, I am a sinner. Yes, I need forgiveness!

Submit yourselves for the Lord's sake to every human authority (1 Peter 2:13).

Let me tell you, I am repentant every day. I could rationalize it in my own mind. After all, it is not murder or theft. So, not so bad, right? The bad news is that if we make it a habit to dismiss the little sins, we will find it easier to rationalize the bigger ones. We all have a tendency to escalate our behaviors. The good news is that with practice we can escalate our good behaviors. I just need to go into strict training.

The first step in defeating our sinful nature is to recognize the sin. When I began paying closer attention to my speedometer, I realized how easily I was breaking the law without even thinking about it. It turns out that technology has been very helpful in this area. It seems my GPS has a speedometer in the corner that turns red when I exceed the posted speed limit. It was extremely difficult at first to stay in the black. However, I found, with persistence and prayer, it was becoming easier. But even more important than my moderate success at following the law, the appearance of that red number on my GPS immediately brings to my mind my heavenly Father and my desire to please Him.

The second step is to practice and pray. Now that the sin has been illuminated, I can consider it a game that I am playing against myself. I will choose to be deliberately obedient to the speed limit. Initially, when I caught myself speeding, I would slow down and ask for the Lord's forgiveness. The problem with just being sorry is that you need to promise to try not to do it again. This did not seem to work for me, as I was repeatedly repenting for the same sin.

> *I do not understand what I do. For what I want to do I do not do, but what I hate I do* (Romans 7:15).

I could just give up and say "Oh well, as a Christian, I am forgiven because of what Christ did for me." Unfortunately, the Bible tells me I need to strive to live better than that. I realized that what I needed was God's help. So now, I have changed my prayer. I simply ask for the Holy Spirit's help in quieting my soul. I am finding this a much more effective way to repent. I am finding that by doing this, I am much more successful. As I glance at the speedometer more frequently, my prayer is one of thanksgiving to God for keeping me in line and helping me to be obedient. It is surprising to me how often I feel I am distracted and driving too fast and I am actually under the speed limit. Thank you, God.

> *God called the light day and the darkness he called night. And there was evening, and there was morning – the first day* (Genesis 1:5).

God created time. I sometimes feel there are not enough hours in a day. I am wrong. There are just the right number of hours, minutes, and seconds in a day. The question is, how am I using the time I have been given? Stress is the by-product of trying to fit too much activity in a short amount of time. The writers of the old Star Trek series imagined it right when they portrayed the characters being transported from one location to another instantaneously via the ionizer. Beam me up, Scottie! That is the ultimate fantasy. If I could travel that way, I would save two to three hours per day! So, what would I do with that extra time each day? Odds are I would find a multitude of things to do or I would do nothing (watch television). In other words, nothing really important. After all, if those things are not getting done now, how important are they really?

> **Thank you, Heavenly Father, for giving me twenty-four hours in a day. I have eight hours to work, eight hours to rest, and eight hours to take care of myself, my home, and my family. Help me to appreciate every minute you have given me, and to avoid both over commitment and laziness.**

Now, a word about appointments. There are several different types of appointments. There are appointments where the activity will not occur unless I am there, such as meeting with clients.

This means that if I am late, someone may have to wait. Most people are pretty understanding if I am running five or ten minutes late. If I am going to be really late, a phone call is the appropriate thing to do. Then, there are appointments where the activity will occur whether I am there on time or not, for example, a church service or staff meeting. While it may be embarrassing to walk in late, it really is not the end of the world. Finally, there are appointments that if I am late, I may not be included at all. This would include missing a bus, train, or plane. Since I rarely take public transportation, these appointments don't generally happen to me. If that is the case, however, I better plan to be early. So now I have convinced myself that time doesn't matter. Yes, time gives order to my day, but it doesn't justify speeding, because after all, how many minutes will I gain by breaking the law?

The most important thing to remember is that God is in control, and if I start to feel out of control, I just need to relax and let God handle it. I find it interesting that all the time I felt there was too much to do and not enough time, I was mistaken. I now find there is plenty of time to do what I need to do, and I even have time to write a book!

> *Love is patient, love is kind. It does not envy, it does not boast, it is not proud. It does not dishonor others, it is not self-seeking, it is not easily angered, it keeps no record of wrongs* (1 Corinthians 13:4–5).

As I said before, I have a wooden cross hanging from my rearview mirror. It has 1 Corinthians 13:4 printed on it. Love is patient (Granny is driving twenty in a thirty-five mph zone!), love is kind (Why should I let you in? It is not my problem you are in the wrong lane), it does not envy (Yeah, I could drive better if I had a sports car), it does not boast (Look at me, I stay under the speed limit, I am a better driver than you). How appropriate is that? Jesus has commanded us to love one another, and Paul instructed us in what that means. So, how do I show love to other drivers? First, I need to recognize who they are. Every driver on the road is either a fellow Christian or a potential Christian. Yes, that crazy driver weaving in and out of traffic could be in heaven with me someday!

Jesus said we should pray for our enemies. Who is more of an enemy than that guy who, with total disregard for my well-being, nearly caused an accident on a busy highway? He is not my enemy because he hates me. He doesn't even know me. He is my enemy because he has no regard for my safety at all. I have no idea why he is behaving that way, and it is not my job to know what is in his heart. I just need to pray for him even when my first instinct is to curse him.

> **May the Lord bless you and keep you. May He make his face shine upon you and be gracious to you. May the Lord lift up His countenance upon you and give you His peace (Numbers 6:24-26).**

I don't know, as I recite the blessing aloud, if the person I am directing it toward feels anything. I do know that I feel the peace of Christ and the power to forgive. The most amazing thing is that the more I practice giving blessings to other drivers the more I feel the desire in my heart for them to feel the peace of God.

Do nothing out of selfish ambition or vain conceit. Rather in humility value others above yourselves, not looking to your own interests but each of you to the interests of others (Philippians 2:3–4).

I remember when I first started trying to be deliberately obedient to the speed limit, I was driving thirty-five mph in a thirty-five mph zone. It was a quiet country road. There were only two of us in sight, me and the guy behind me tailgating and blowing his horn. I remember thinking *I am not going to allow you to intimidate me into speeding.* Upon reflection, however, I realize that I was not showing love to this man. I was being cocky in my attitude. I have always struggled with this particular *trapping* of my spiritual nature. I decided that if that situation should present itself again, the loving thing to do would be to pull over and allow the other driver to pass. After all, I do not know the reason he is behaving that way, and it is not my business to judge him.

It is important to note that the evil within can easily turn something good into self-serving ugliness. I must constantly remind myself that giving a blessing to another driver is in no way a criticism of their driving skills. It is not my job to judge them, only to pray that they will feel the peace of Christ in their lives.

> *"Then your Father who sees what is done in secret will reward you"* (Matthew 6:6).

We are commanded to love our neighbor as ourselves. The parable of the Good Samaritan tells us that our neighbor is anyone we encounter. So this would include all the people driving beside, in front, or behind me. It could also include the people whose homes I am driving past.

I noticed a sign in front of a home I was passing that simply read *speed kills*. It reminded me of how angry my mother would get when someone would be speeding down our street as her children were outside playing. She would frequently threaten to buy some cement and build a speed bump in the middle of the road. I sometimes imagine the people in the homes as I drive through a residential area. I often ask God to help me show love to these people by respecting their neighborhood. Again, I do not know, as it is not my responsibility to know, what is in their hearts, I just need to show them kindness and respect whether they are aware of it or not.

I find it interesting that one would think I would reach a point with all this practicing, that I would actually achieve the goal I set out to accomplish. This is not the case. I am finding that, although some days are easier than others, I can see that I need God to help me to control my behavior every day. And this will be a lifelong need. In other words, I am learning to include God in my daily life and it will never end. Complete obedience was never really the goal. Convincing myself I need God every minute of my day was. Goal met

Praise God. He will never leave me!

Chapter 5

THE CONSEQUENCES

Then we will no longer be infants, tossed back and forth by the waves, and blown here and there by every wind of teaching and by the cunning and craftiness of people in their deceitful scheming. Instead, speaking the truth in love, we will grow to become in every respect the mature body of him who is the head, that is the Christ (Ephesians 4:14–15).

The preacher says "a moment of silence to confess our sins to God...either specific sins or just a general confession of our sinfulness." I hear it quite frequently, and I have said it myself, "I am a sinner." I agree that we must admit our sinfulness, but I find that *general confession* feels meaningless.

To say I am a sinner without recalling specific sins and truly being sorry for them leaves my heart feeling empty. How can I feel forgiven if I don't admit my transgressions? While it is difficult to admit my real sins, it is a very necessary step in the growth process. I must feel sorrow to feel grace. How can I turn from my sinful ways if I don't recognize them? By practicing recognizing my sin while driving has given me a greater discernment of my behaviors. And, therefore, a greater appreciation for the power of forgiveness.

In my youth, I used to think "If it were me, I would not have eaten from the tree of knowledge of good and evil" or "If it were me, I would not have denied Jesus three times." The reality is that every time I am disobedient or judge others, I am eating the forbidden fruit. And every time I gossip or say a hurtful thing to others, I am denying Christ. The difference between Judas' sin and Peter's sin on the night of Jesus' arrest is the matter of the heart. Judas' sorrow was focused inward (ego) and how the events affected him, and therefore, he could not feel forgiveness. Peter, on the other hand, felt sorrow outside of himself, focusing on how the events affected Jesus and the other followers. Peter did feel the forgiveness, and therefore remained a devoted follower of Christ. We know how things turned out for Judas.

God is an emotional being. The Bible cites various occasions when God was angry, joyful, sad, etc. He created us in his image, and we are emotional beings. Emotions are not a bad thing. It does become a problem when we allow our emotions to control our behavior. That is not to say that we should not act on our emotions particularly if it is in defense of another or to encourage one another. We should, however, keep our emotions in check. We need to make sure what we are feeling is justified. We need to analyze what we are feeling and why (Is it self-serving?), and then respond accordingly. By actively sending a blessing aloud to other drivers who are, in my opinion, being reckless or rude, I am focusing my attention away from what I am feeling and asking God to intervene in what they are feeling. It brings my focus away from myself and back to God.

> *Then he said to them all: Whoever wants to be my disciple must deny themselves and take up their cross daily and follow me* (Luke 9:23).

It is not an easy task to deny your own feelings in the car. It means that whatever emotion I am feeling must be set aside while I concentrate on following the rules of the road. As I practice deliberate obedience while driving, I am finding it easier to recognize the effects my emotions have on my behavior in this and other situations. I do, however, recognize the fact that as a sinful human being, I need to continually ask God to help me control my emotional responses.

Chapter 6

FINAL THOUGHTS

Endure hardship as discipline; God is treating you as his children (Hebrews 12:7).

It is important to remember that the goal is total reliance on God. The purpose being not to feel superior or pious, but weak and needy. By practicing self-denial, we become more aware of the needs of others and the power of God. If deliberate obedience while driving is not a challenge for you, there are other ways to work toward the goal. The point is to take a routine—

an everyday task—and deliberately make it more difficult to increase your reliance on God.

The following is an outline of another way to make a routine task more difficult for the glory of God:

> *For physical training is of some value, but godliness has value for all things, holding promise for both the present life and the life to come* (1 Timothy 4:8).

Most people understand that our physical fitness is directly related to the food we eat and the exercise we give our bodies. The junk food-eating couch potato is not going to be as fit as the athlete. Are either of them satisfied with the degree of fitness of their bodies? No. There is no ultimate level of fitness that, once reached, you can stop trying. Eventually, the human body breaks down. It is a fact of life. Does that mean that we should not even try? Of course not. We have a responsibility to take care of the body God has given us, however, not at the expense of our spiritual selves. I have developed for myself a routine of doing yoga while praying.

1. While holding plank pose, I thank God for the strength and flexibility of my body. I contemplate the fact that he has designed the human body to respond to exercise and improve upon itself.

2. I recite the Lord's Prayer as a member of the church body (traditional recitation) while holding tree pose:

   Our Father who art in heaven, hallowed be thy name. Thy kingdom come, thy will be done on earth as it is in heaven. Give us this day our daily bread and forgive us our trespasses as we forgive those who trespass against us. And lead us not into temptation, but deliver us from evil. For thine is the kingdom, the power and the glory forever and ever. Amen.

3. Then in a more personal way, while holding dancer pose:

   My Father who is in heaven, holy is your name. Your kingdom come, your will be done, in my life as it is in heaven. Give me this day, my daily

word, and forgive me my sins as I forgive those who have hurt me. And keep me strong against temptation and protect me from every evil. For Yours is the kingdom, and Yours is the power, and Yours is the glory, forever and ever. Amen.

The idea of changing and alternating the words of the Lord's Prayer was to confuse my mind so that I was forced to think about what I was saying.

4. I use the time in child's pose for intercessions. I pray for those who are in need—my family and my friends. I then pray for myself. I ask God to affect my heart with whatever virtue I am feeling particularly lacking—wisdom, generosity, forgiveness etc. I am constantly amazed at how quickly these prayers are answered. I had a coworker who hurt me. The anger was overwhelming and lasted a very long time. I could not imagine ever forgiving her. It was shortly after asking God to put forgiveness in my heart that suddenly, I felt great love for her and now consider her one of my best friends.

My initial reason for doing this was to save time and make the prayer more meaningful. I wanted to use my body and mind simultaneously to praise God. By multitasking exercise and prayer, I have found that I have the added benefit of dual motivation. My need to exercise motivates me to pray, and my need to pray motivates me to exercise. I am finding there are many less days that I am talking myself out of doing this routine.

Many years ago, I was working in a small town in southern Ohio. On Sundays, I attended a small Lutheran Church. One week, there was a prayer by an unknown author printed in the worship folder that touched me. I copied that prayer, framed it, and read it from time to time:

I asked for strength that I might achieve;
I was made weak that I might learn to humbly obey…

I asked for health, that I might do greater things;
I was given infirmity that I might do better things…

I asked for riches that I might be happy;
I was given poverty, that I might be wise…

I asked for power, that I might have the praise
    of men;
I was given weakness that I might feel the need for
    God…

I ask for all things, that I might enjoy life;
I was given life that I might enjoy all things…

I got nothing I asked for but everything I hoped for…

Almost despite myself, my unspoken prayers were
    answered.
I am among men most richly blessed!

Jesus looked at them and said With man this is impossible, but with God all things are possible (Matthew 19:26).

Even though it is not in our nature to seek to make our lives more difficult, the rewards are unimaginable. I am often looking for ways to challenge myself spiritually. I don't want to give away all of my secrets (I want the promised treasures in heaven). I don't want to allow myself to feel spiritually superior to others (for only God knows what's in the heart), and each person needs to find their own spiritual challenges. I pray that you will find value in my challenge, and that you will ask God to show you the way and let Him guide your journey.

> *And the peace of God, which transcends all understanding, will guard your hearts and minds in Christ Jesus* (Philippians 4:7).